raising a
happy
confident
successful
child

52 lessons to help parents grow

Trish Magee

ADAMS MEDIA CORPORATION
Holbrook, Massachusetts

*To June Muller, my mother, and Grace Magee,
my mother-in-law, whose dedication and love of
parenting is well reflected in the pages that follow.*

Published by
Adams Media Corporation
260 Center Street, Holbrook, MA 02343

Editorial Assistant: Marc Magee. Cover Design: Mitchell Magee

ISBN: 1-55850-836-8

Printed in Canada.

J I H G F E D C B A

Library of Congress Cataloging-in-Publication Data
Magee, Trish.
Raising a happy confident successful child : 52 lessons to help parents grow /
by Trish Magee.
p.   cm.
Originally published : Philadelphia : Spencer Books, 1996.
ISBN 1-55850-836-8
1. Parent and child. 2. Parenting. I. Title.
HQ755.85.M254   1998
649'.1—dc21   97–39261
CIP

This book is available at quantity discounts for bulk purchases.
For information, call 1-800-872-5627 (in Massachusetts, 781-767-8100).

Visit our home page at http://www.adamsmedia.com

• • TABLE OF CONTENTS • •

• • INTRODUCTION • •

I grew up in a family of 10 children. I had an early start on parenting because my father died when I was 10 years old. As one of the oldest children I quickly found myself drawn toward helping my mom care for my younger brothers and sisters since she had to take three jobs to make ends meet. What started as a responsibility turned into a lifelong interest as I set about making up games and projects for my siblings. This in turn resulted in my first career move. When I was 13 years old I created the Candy Cane Camp for the neighborhood children and charged parents 75 cents a week for their children to attend, obviously lacking any business sense.

After several years of teaching kindergarten and first grade, my husband Mike and I started a family of our own. During those years of our family life my interest in parenting switched from an academic one to something more personal. I reveled in the nitty-gritty of everyday parenting and, together with some friends, I set up a playgroup for our children. Mike and I had three boys, Michael, Mitch and Marc, in a four-year period. What I remember most about those early years is action. The boys were always moving and they forced me to think on my feet as together we developed projects and activities to keep up with their curiosity and energy. A few years later, our fourth child, Meredith, was born. She was the perfect addition to the family and at last, after three boys, Meredith made the family complete. Together our four children continually sparked my interest in parenting and I began to share this interest with other parents through workshops and publications.

Many years later, while I was supervising student teachers, I reflected on how much the information I taught students was similar to the workshops I had conducted for parents of young children years before. This observation led to the development of an Early Learning Center with parenting workshops located at a health clinic for parents on public assistance in Philadelphia. These workshops, along with the recent milestones of watching my oldest son get married and my youngest child go off to high school, have led me to focus on the many parenting experiences I have had and all the people I have met since I began this journey 40 years ago as a young girl with new challenges and responsibilities. The focus on the stories from my life and the lives of friends and family became the foundation for this book.

The lessons presented here are derived from everyday experiences. They are presented in five themes: Listen and Learn, Support, Involve, Plan and Enjoy. Each theme is illustrated with 10 principles, each with its own story and quote. Taken as a whole they represent a life's work, since they are the result of the wisdom and experience of all the people whom I have met on this journey. Some principles will be easier to adopt than others. You may find out that you already possess many of the qualities presented here. If so, I hope that this book helps strengthen those principles and gives you confidence in your parenting. However, if there is anything that I have discovered about parenting it is that you never stop growing because there is always something new to learn.

• • •

Theme #1
LISTEN AND LEARN

The best home environments are dynamic ones because they nourish personal growth and development. Small children always contribute to this kind of environment since they have a natural instinct to explore their world. They possess the two most important qualities needed for learning: curiosity and energy. These qualities drive children to ask questions and these questions become windows to different worlds. The easiest way for parents to become motivated to learn is simply to spend time with their children. But the principle of "Listen and Learn" is more than just exploring with your children. Listening is taking time out to appreciate someone else, whether that person is your child or simply another parent you admire. When you begin to look for people to learn from, you will find they are all around you. For wherever there is diversity there is a chance for growth.

• • •

•• 1 ••

See the Goodness

"Eden is that old-fashioned House
We dwell in every day;
Without suspecting our abode
Until we drive away."
— *Emily Dickinson*

It's easy to get caught up in focusing on the negative. Maybe you didn't get a good night's sleep or you're under a lot of stress or you're just feeling under the weather. It's at these times that we can all start to see only the bad things and lose sight of the special kindness all around us every day in our homes.

Like many American families we have had to move several times with our children. As any family who has gone through this knows, it can be emotionally traumatic for the entire family. When Meredith was 7 years old we moved to Longmeadow, Massachusetts in September just as the school year was starting. Both Marc, who was going into seventh grade, and Mitchell, who was starting high school, had a difficult time adjusting. But the move was especially difficult for Meredith. By the time Halloween had rolled around Meredith had not made a close friend for trick-or-treating. It had always been a tradition in our family to make a big deal out of Halloween and I had made a homemade costume for her. Mike had told her it would be fun if he went with her, but clearly Meredith was upset over not having made a friend yet.

I woke up on Halloween with a big headache. I had been tossing and turning all night long. I dragged myself out of bed and went downstairs for a cup of coffee. Soon Mike joined me and then, a few minutes later, Meredith, Marc and Michael came into the kitchen for breakfast. I looked up at the clock and realized we were running late. "Where's Mitchell?" No one answered so I went up to his room and found him fast asleep. There was paper everywhere from the homework he had been working on the night before and it covered up the dirty clothes that were on the floor. "Mitch!" I shouted. "Wake up!" His eyes fluttered open, but he was only partially aware of his surroundings. "Wake up! We're already late . . . and clean up this room!" I went back downstairs, muttering to myself.

That night Meredith ate her dinner quietly, slowly mulling over the food. After dinner, as I was helping Meredith put on her costume, Mitch could see how glum she was about walking around with her dad on Halloween night. Without saying a word, he went upstairs and put together a wild-looking costume and within minutes announced that he would love to go trick-or-treating with her. I know there was a level at which Mitch was totally embarrassed to be walking around trick-or-treating with his little sister, but I'm eternally grateful that he sucked in all his teenage pride and self-consciousness to make sure that his sister didn't feel badly that Halloween night.

I had started the day focusing on Mitchell's negatives. I had concentrated so much on his messiness and his lateness that I nearly forgot what I loved so much about him: his courage, his kindness and his thoughtfulness. His positive qualities far outweighed any shortcomings, but by dwelling only on the negatives I had almost missed them.

• • •

·· 2 ··

Be a Model

"Children have never been very good at listening to their elders, but they have never failed to imitate them."
—*James Baldwin*

Children are always studying the world around them. Most of what they learn comes from observation and in their early years the people they observe the most are their parents. Therefore, if you want to teach your child something, simply be a good model.

It was one of those days. I was having a "terrible, rotten, no good, very bad day." You know the scenario. As soon as you get one child settled down another gets riled up. Complaints and requests fly at you from every direction. That morning while Marc and Meredith ran around the house playing with action heroes and Michael was unloading all of the fruit from the refrigerator looking for the exact orange he wanted, Mitchell had set his mind on painting and decided that at that very minute he absolutely needed paints set up. In a very loud, demanding voice he barked off his orders, "Get my paints down!"

I turned around and in an even louder, more bellowing voice responded, "Where did you get that loud, obnoxious voice?" Everyone stopped what they were doing and for a brief moment there was absolute silence. Mitchell looked at me, scratching his head, and said, "I wonder where I got that loud, obnoxious voice?"

• • •

Learn From Others

"You can observe a lot just by watching."
— *Yogi Berra*

Observation requires a certain amount of humility. In order to learn from someone we have to stop what we're doing, free ourselves from the impulse to butt in, and just watch.

After raising four children and obtaining two advanced degrees in early childhood education over the course of 20 years, I felt like I knew a great deal about parenting. That was until I met a women named Donna. I was conducting summer playgroups for parents at a pediatric clinic. Donna had signed up for the playgroup for infants and asked if her four older children might attend since she didn't have anyone to watch them while she attended the playgroup sessions. I had entered into the summer playgroup thinking I would be able to share a lot of parenting information. But I soon realized that this would be a learning opportunity for me as well. I found myself stopping what I was doing and observing how Donna spoke to her children. I was amazed by the way she made eye contact with them and reassured her children with her gentle voice. Over the course of the next eight weeks my assistant and I witnessed the most loving, gentle mother we had ever seen and that love was reflected in the most confident, caring, interested and happy children we had ever met.

During my training as a teacher I learned the importance of not disciplining children by yelling, but sometimes all theory went out the window when my emotions got the best of me while disciplining my own kids. When I watched Donna, however, the theory came to life. There it was that summer, living proof that firm yet gentle discipline really worked. We watched Donna speak softly to her nine and ten-year-old boys when she didn't like what they were doing and reminded them of the consequences if they did not rethink their actions. She taught them cooperation and responsibility and we witnessed all her children helping to gather their belongings after each session, each older child taking a younger child by the hand. Their father, Mike, would pick them up after work exhibiting the same patient parenting skills: the gentle touch and the reassuring voice. Soon all the parents in the playgroup, along with my assistants and I, looked to Mike and Donna for a better understanding of how to parent.

Donna and Mike, who have worked against the odds in raising their children in the projects of Philadelphia, now conduct the positive discipline workshops at our pediatric clinic. I rarely yell anymore, and when I need reassurance I just stop and watch Donna. There are many people to learn from in the world. All you have to do is keep your eyes and your mind open.

• • •

• • 4 • •

Be Respectful

*"Man does not live on bread alone. Many prefer
self-respect to food."*
— *Mohandas K. Gandhi*

Sometimes we tend to think of respect as a one-way street.
Children, it is often said, should be respectful of their
elders. It is curious that this doesn't seem to work both
ways. How often is it said that elders must respect their
children? Yet that is exactly what must take place if you are
to create a loving environment for your child.

Respect, in its fully developed form, is more than just
politeness, it is an understanding of a person's place in the
world. When children are told to respect their elders what
they are really being asked to do is appreciate where they are
coming from. They should understand the sacrifices their
parents and grandparents have made for them and the challenges they have overcome to get to where they are today.
Children should appreciate the wisdom that experience carries with it. Just as children should respect their elders, parents should learn to respect their children. In order to cre-

ate an appropriate environment for your children you should try to appreciate where they are coming from and what they are capable of at each point in their development. You should be aware that children often speak with great honesty and clarity. You should always keep in mind that something that they might say could provide you with valuable insight.

I remember overhearing a conversation my brother-in-law had with his dad some years back. His dad had said that his grandchildren never kiss him when he arrives for visits. Bill replied, "Dad, you have to remember that they're very young and at this age they can be very shy. Sometimes they need you to go up and say hello to them before they warm up." It was such simple advice, but it demonstrates that understanding children can make all the difference in a relationship. For example, most parents understand that their children's smaller legs make it more difficult for them to keep up. When parents slow their pace they are showing respect for their child's situation. This simple act demonstrates a larger principle: it is important that parents take time to think through where their children are coming from and in doing so make respect a two-way street.

• • •

Be Consistent

"Consistency is like flossing your teeth. You have to do it every day. Flossing like crazy on the weekends doesn't work."
— *Ada Alden*

Without consistency, what can you count on? Dealing with change is one of the major stresses in life. When you think about the first two decades of a person's life, those years are filled with the greatest change. Our minds, our bodies, our relationships, our hopes and our dreams change day by day. To survive and thrive in the middle of all that change, it's extremely important that children be able to count on some things staying the same in those early years.

I'll never forget the first time I met my mother-in-law. I was 16 years old and Mike had brought me to his house to meet his large family. As we walked in the door, Mike started to introduce me to his mom but there was so much noise she couldn't hear what he was saying. She turned to her large brood and in a soft but firm voice said, "Cease the din." At the time, I thought she must be putting on a show because there was a new person in the house. But as I began to spend more and more time at their home I soon discovered this was her consistent way of disciplining. I've known my mother-in-law for 32 years now and I am still amazed that I never once heard her yell at her children.

I think one of the greatest gifts she gave her children was a very secure home environment. They could count on her temperament (always even), her discipline (firm but fair), her time (if she said she would be there to pick them up she was there right on time), her routines (homemade meals, everything in its place), her values ("no fraternizing in the bedroom") and her love (for them and their father). Their home was anchored in consistent parenting behavior. It was the security blanket within which they were raised.

Building predictability not only means holding the line in areas such as discipline. It means creating a structure of routine pleasures that one can anticipate, like pizza on Friday night, a bedtime story, or a TV show you watch together.

• • •

•• 6 ••

Be Courageous

"Courage is the ladder on which all other virtues mount."
— Claire Booth Luce

One of the qualities that seems to routinely come with parenting is increased vulnerability. No matter how secure a person you are, it seems impossible not to worry about your children. Are they safe? Will they make friends? Will they get ill? The truth is that parenting can worry you half to death. That's why parents need courage.

My sister, Priscilla, received a call one day on the job announcing that her perfectly healthy daughter, Maria, had had a seizure. "Meet us at the hospital" was the message. You can imagine how she felt as she rushed to her child's side. And for the following two weeks, you can understand the stress of multiple exams, blood tests and CAT scan attempts on a child whose body seemed to respond paradoxically to sedation. When the tests showed epilepsy, Priscilla had to be the one to reassure day care teachers, friends and relatives. Next she and her husband, Tom, took on the task of creating reliable techniques to get Maria's daily medicine into her. And finally there was the task of normalizing their home again and reassuring Maria's brother, James. That took a lot of courage.

Where did that courage come from? Probably from my mother's example of being so strong and steady after my father's death when we were young children. Parents underestimate their strength at times of crisis. "It's too scary," many might say. And sometimes it is. But the mystery is that parents and children in overwhelming numbers prevail and enrich each others' lives.

• • •

Make Kindness the Norm

"Kindness and generosity form the true morality of human actions."

— *Madame de Stael*

Often in our society we elevate certain acts of kindness to heroic proportions. On one level this is helpful since it brings attention to the good that these acts bring. However, an unfortunate result of this glorification of only the most dramatic acts of kindness is that it reinforces the idea that kindness should be viewed as something rare and unusual. Children are always gathering information in an attempt to understand their world. Perhaps the lesson children learn from the way the media treats these rare acts is that one doesn't have to be kind all the time, that an extraordinary act more than makes up for any shortcomings. In our continuing search for the big story we often lose sight of the simple acts of kindness that take place every day.

I had a great aunt whose nickname was Toddles. She never married and so my mother's big brood of 10 children became a great source of entertainment and companionship for her. She often came over for dinner and afterward we would sit around as she captivated us with her stories and we entertained her with our little skits. As my brothers and sisters and I got married and had children we continued to celebrate with Toddles. She enjoyed the energy that our children showed as they ran and played around my mother's house on Thanksgiving and Christmas. As the years rolled by it became necessary to place Aunt Toddles in a nursing home. The next Thanksgiving we simply moved the celebration to the nursing home where the children played in her room as we reminisced with Toddles about the past. We would sing songs and the children would dance. Too often when people grow old they are excluded from activities even though they still have much to share. We did not tell our children that they were participating in an unusual act of kindness. Celebrating in the nursing home became what was expected because kindness became the norm.

• • •

•• 8 ••

Be A Good Listener

*"If you love to hear, you will
receive,
And if you listen, you will be
wise."*

—Ben Sira

When you grow up in a family of 10 children, as I did, you get used to having several conversations at once. It's easy to grow up thinking you are an excellent communicator without realizing you may not be the best listener.

My friend Ann's strength was that she was a listener. You never felt rushed or hurried when sharing your thoughts, opinions or comments with her. I was moved by the importance of this characteristic many years ago when I witnessed an emotional interchange between Ann and her young son, Jed. Their family had just been blessed with a new arrival, an adopted sister for Jed.

Jed was 5 years old and was sitting with his mother at the kitchen table making peanut butter sandwiches when he said "Mom" in a soft voice. Ann stopped what she was doing and looked at him. You could see him relax as he stared at her gentle smile. "Mom, I'm glad we adopted Susanna because now I don't have to pretend I have a sister anymore. I used to tell everyone in school I had a sister but now I don't have to make believe." Ann smiled and simply said, "I'm glad too." She knew this was a time for listening. There were no lectures at this time on telling the truth, what's real or not real. There were no questions like, "Did you tell your teacher you had a sister?" She simply allowed her child to share his innermost thoughts without being criticized or judged.

There's a difference between hearing and listening. Hearing requires a moderate level of awareness and can be done even if you're distracted by external events or internal thoughts. Listening, on the other hand, requires that you be still and fully engaged. Children need us to listen in order for them to grow.

• • •

• • 9 • •

Grow With Your Children

"The greatest lessons in life, if we would but stoop and humble ourselves, we would learn not from the grown-up learned men, but from the so-called ignorant children."
— *Mohandas K. Gandhi*

Children seem to have a thirst for life. They are always exploring new places and asking questions in an effort to understand their world. As parents we often think that it is the child's job to learn and our job to teach. But if you let them, children can make you excited about learning with them.

When we lived in North Carolina, Michael had an unquenchable curiosity for all the animals that lived in and around the creek in our backyard. One hot summer day as I was preparing dinner, Michael, age 5, came into the kitchen and tapped me on the shoulder. As I turned around he asked calmly, "Mom, what kind of a snake is this?" There was Michael, wide-eyed, holding a huge black snake and wondering about its name and classification. I let out a blood-curdling scream and jumped up on a chair. However, after I got over the initial shock, we looked at the snake's characteristics, put it back near the creek and went off to the library to look it up in a snake book. Before Michael was born I couldn't describe the difference between an oak leaf or a maple leaf, a hermit crab or a horseshoe crab. But his energy and enthusiasm got me interested in all sorts of subjects. During the five years we lived in North Carolina, I think I learned the name of every plant and animal in the area.

As parents, Mike and I have had the privilege of watching our children grow as they acquired more and more knowledge of their surroundings. But when I look back on these years I can't believe how much we've learned and grown through our children. Each of our children has introduced us to something different. Mitchell has drawn us into the world of art. Michael has helped us understand and enjoy poetry. Through Marc's enthusiasm we've explored all aspects of science, technology, space and politics. Finally, Meredith has raised our awareness of animal rights, food and nutrition, and the wonder of the world of nature. If you share in their excitement, your children can open up whole new worlds for you.

• • •

•• 10 ••

Set Limits

"Self-reliance comes about after establishing a sense of personal security. Kids need reassurance that they are loved. If they don't have limits they don't feel loved and they look for it some place else."

— *Ada Alden*

Children seem to be naturally drawn to extremes. It's a way of testing the limits of safety, of endurance, of rules and of themselves. It can be very confusing for parents of toddlers, pre-adolescents or teens. The "final-straw request" is really just their way of saying, "Have I reached the limit?"

During Marc's early years as a teenager he seemed to be a whirlwind of social activities, constantly making plans for athletic events, concerts or pick-up games with his friends. We seemed to be regularly at odds with his social agenda. One night, he arrived an hour after his curfew without having called. Rather than discuss it when we were upset, we told him to go to bed and we'd talk about it in the morning. We decided we needed some limits to his never-ending schedule. The next day, we sat down with Marc and came up with an agreement together. We created a calendar for the remaining eight weeks of the summer. Each week, we allowed him two late nights until 11 pm and two early nights until 9:30 pm. Friends could visit at our house anytime. He would mark an "L" for a late night and an "E" for an early night. To our surprise he liked the idea of choosing his nights out and the rest of the summer went smoothly. We put it in writing so we both remembered what we had agreed on and set up consequences if the agreement was broken.

Parents often underestimate their children's need for limits and their ability to find comfort in structured boundaries. The absence of limits forces children into behavior that might otherwise not be necessary.

• • •

Theme #2
SUPPORT

The secret ingredient in all successful human endeavors is support. This is especially true for parenting. Support is not just a tool of parenting, but a guiding philosophy. It is a principle built on personal relationships and trust. It values cooperation and communication between friends and neighbors, between a husband and wife, and between parents and their children. The network of support you develop will allow you to better enjoy your role as a parent and will help you create the best possible environment for your child. However, support is not just what friends and family members can give to parents, it is also a precious gift that parents can give to their children. The support a parent gives to a child can take many forms. Sometimes it takes the form of a hug. Other times your support calls for you to stand up and be an advocate for your child. Whatever form your support takes the message you send your child is always the same: I love you and will always be here for you.

• • •

•• 11 ••

Be Accepting

"If children live with approval, they learn to live with themselves."

— *Dorothy Law Nolte*

Sometimes parents focus so much on what they want for their children that they forget to ask what their child thinks. In their quest to guide their children through life, parents can drown out their child's individuality.

Ten years ago, I set out on my daughter Meredith's bed the nicest plaid jumper, a cute little Peter-Pan-collared blouse and Mary Jane shoes with white tights. It was her first day of kindergarten and I picked out the perfect "first day of school" outfit. I went downstairs, loaded my camera, put on a pot of coffee and waited. This was one of those milestone days that I wanted to capture on film. I was sending my last child off to kindergarten. I looked up at the clock and realized it was almost time to leave for school. I called to Meredith and told her it was time to get dressed for school. "I'm already dressed," she shouted from the living room. I walked into the living room and there she stood in a pink- and-purple-striped blouse with a white pair of pants and white sandals. Thinking that she must have missed the outfit I had laid out for her, I told her to go upstairs and put on the new outfit in her room. "But I already picked out what I want to wear," she exclaimed. "I think you should wear the jumper on your first day," I said in my best motherly tone. As she lowered her head she said, "But, mom, I like to wear pants." This was her first day of school and I was making her feel badly. "You're right," I said, "the white pants are perfect."

I look back on the pictures I took that day and there is Meredith beaming with confidence surrounded by all her girl friends in dresses, jumpers and skirts. I had learned the hard way to accept the decisions our children make that have nothing to do with right or wrong, good or bad. I look back at the hard times I gave Mitch because I thought his hair was too long. Here was Mitch, a conscientious high school student whom his teachers and friends admired, and I was nagging him constantly about the length of his hair. When parents are confronted with a difference of opinion from their child it is important to take a step back and ask yourself what's at stake. Your children are not you, they are individuals and sometimes it's necessary to be accepting when they have a different opinion.

• • •

•• 12 ••

Be an Advocate

"One must be slow to form convictions, but once formed, they must be defended against the heaviest odds."
— *Mohandas K. Gandhi*

As parents, we all have the responsibility of supporting our children by coming to their aid in times of need. Sometimes situations arise where children are unable to defend themselves and it is then that they need their parents' support the most.

We've been blessed with four unique children, with four very different personalities. Mitchell, our second child, likes to take his time when doing a task and thinks long and hard before he starts anything. He always has had these characteristics, even when he was very little.

When Mitchell was 7 years old he came home on the second day of school and said that his teacher had told him he was "lazy." He explained that he hadn't finished any of his dittos and his teacher thought he was not trying very hard. My husband, Mike, has always been an advocate for the children and this time was no exception.

The next morning he asked to speak to Mitch's teacher. He told her that we understood that Mitchell sometimes took longer than the other children to do his work, but that he always worked hard and was not lazy. He said that one of Mitchell's special qualities was that he spent a long time on tasks and did his work slowly, but deliberately, to make sure he did the job right. They agreed that it would be more constructive if, instead of labeling Mitchell, she worked with him on strategies to help him complete his tasks on time.

There are many times when we all must go to bat for our children. Teachers and other people in your child's world can make mistakes and sometimes the environment your child is placed into isn't a constructive one. No one likes confrontation, but if you speak up on behalf of your child, and do it with a sense of fairness and respect, it almost always results in a positive outcome for your child.

• • •

•• 13 ••

Persevere

"To keep a lamp burning, we have to keep putting oil in it."
— *Mother Teresa*

Sometimes the best technique for parenting is just to keep trying. Many problems and disappointments will arise throughout the lives of your children. There is no way to avoid this because it is part of life, but what you can do instead is view these problems as challenges. With this new frame of mind, the problems become less formidable and you become motivated to persevere.

Our first child, Michael, has always been the talker in our family. He began speaking when he was very young and hasn't stopped since. As a child he could never have enough stories read to him each night. This love of stories helped him learn the letters of the alphabet quickly and he was only too happy to demonstrate this skill to anyone who would listen. Therefore, it was really quite surprising that by the end of first grade he was still struggling with learning how to read. Every day I would sit down with him and work on reading from one of the classic early readers. Once a week I would take him to the library and we would take out a new early-reader book, but nothing seemed to work. We returned week after week having made no progress with the latest book.

Finally, one hot summer day, we got in the car and drove down to the local library as we had every week for the last few months. As we walked through the children's section I began to wonder if all of this effort was useless, and then from behind a bookshelf I heard Michael shout, "Mom, I want to take out this book!" He was holding in his hand a book from a series called *Dan Frontier*. Don't ask me why, but Michael loved these stories and because he was interested in what they had to say he tried with all his might to figure out what each word meant. Well, that did it. He quickly taught himself how to read as he finished book after book in the series. As the summer ended and he began school again, he had become one of the strongest readers in his class. I sometimes wonder what would have happened if we hadn't continued to go back to the library week after week. Would Michael be pursuing his doctorate in English right now? When you are confronted with challenges the best technique is usually to just keep on trying.

• • •

•• 14 ••

Make the Time

"I must govern the clock, not be governed by it."
— *Golda Meir*

No one needs to remind us what a fast-paced world we live in. Free time seems to shrink more and more every year. Today, the time parents do manage to free up for their children always seems to be spent hurrying from one place to another, from one event to the other. This is especially true for the millions of households with children where both parents work. But child development can't be rushed. Despite the challenges of the modern-day schedule, parents must recommit themselves to making the time.

Our third child, Marc, defies that fast-paced, modern-day mind set. He is our "spirited child" and has always had an enormous intensity for everything he does. He always dreams big and soon finds himself involved in all sorts of projects that require a lot of time and a lot of patience. So we always took a deep breath when he approached us with a request for assistance in completing one of his projects.

When Marc was in the third grade he decided it would be fun to start his own classroom newspaper. He got permission from his teacher, created an initial design of what the paper would look like, and then set out to convince his dad that this would be a great thing to do together. Although Mike was just starting up a busy private practice in surgery and didn't think he had the time, he agreed to help. Marc went about encouraging classmates to contribute and with Mike's help constructed contribution boxes that were placed in every classroom. At the end of every month the "Owl News" box was filled with classmates' drawings, jokes and stories. Marc would empty out the boxes and on Saturday Mike would take him to his office where they would put the issue together. They would work all Saturday cutting, pasting and photocopying and on Monday morning Marc would walk into school with 50 new copies of the newspaper for his classmates.

There have been other projects over the years – go-carts, magic light boxes, and animated stop-action films – where we've somehow managed to set aside a quantity of time to support Marc in his constant quest for learning, inventing, creating and imagining. Marc is a senior in college now and who knows where all of this creative energy will take him. But I really believe the Steven Spielbergs of the world had a parent supporting and encouraging their projects during their childhood.

• • •

•• 15 ••

Be Understanding

"He who forgives ends the quarrel."
— *African saying*

Arguments can start over the most trivial things: a lost remote control, whose turn it is to do the dishes or whose turn is next in a card game. Once accusations are made people find it very difficult to take them back. This can cause very trivial arguments to grow into problems and everyone involved ends up feeling badly. It is important to make people feel comfortable apologizing if a mistake is made or an accusation turns out to be false. If a family is quick to forgive and forget, trivial arguments simply disappear.

I can't explain how a line from a Gilda Radner character on *Saturday Night Live* infiltrated our family life, but it has helped provide a face-saving way to defuse disputes and misunderstandings. Here's how it works in our family. We've all experienced a situation where you insist that you are right about something and that everyone else must be conspiring against you and then find out later that you were wrong. Rather than going around making awkward retractions and apologies you simply say, in Gilda Radner's voice, "Never mind." Simply put, this means you're sorry you accused them wrongly.

Once our third child, Marc, could not find the remote control and went around interrogating everyone in the family about where *they* had put it last. After an exhaustive search he went to the refrigerator to get a drink only to realize that there, between the orange juice and leftover pasta, was the remote. This jogged his memory and to his embarrassment he realized that he had accidentally left it there when he had gotten a snack while watching television. No one likes to admit they are wrong, but a simple "Never mind" said it all. We all shared a laugh and then the argument disappeared. By providing a way for people to save face, while still apologizing, you can save a lot of bruised egos and stop problems before they start.

• • •

•• 16 ••

Be Compassionate

"There never was any heart truly great and generous that was not also tender and compassionate."
—*Robert South*

Children have so much to learn that it's remarkable how well they do most of the time. A parent's challenge is to lay the ground work for a secure, compassionate relationship with their child.

It had been a long day at our Ready to Learn Camp. It was the first day for a group of inner city children experiencing what it was like to be in a school setting before they started Kindergarten. I couldn't believe the number of times I had to remind some of the children to keep their hands at their sides, to walk slowly and not push anyone.

As the children were gathering their belongings, I heard a loud thump. Donovan and Joshua were both on the ground, rubbing their heads and crying. They had been wrestling and lost their balance and crashed to the ground. At that moment, the last thing I wanted to do was to comfort each with a hug, but as a teacher I have learned that responding to misbehavior with an angry outburst does *not* teach a child how to behave. I put my arms around each of them as I spoke to them of the dangers of their behavior. I asked each to apologize to the other, and we talked about the consequences if it happened again. They both listened to me because they knew I cared and because and there was no anger in my voice. I was there to help them.

Of course, there were other episodes throughout the summer, but I saw Donovan and Joshua grow more and more responsible for their behavior as the weeks went by. I saw progress, not perfection.

Over the years, I have witnessed many different responses from parents whose children have made mistakes. One parent comforts a child who wets his pants. The child knows the consequences of having an accident. It feels wet and cold against his leg. Another parent, facing an identical situation, responds with an angry voice and spanking. The child is left humiliated and hurt after having failed.

It is so important to establish a compassionate relationship when your children are young! Your patience and guidance will really pay off during the teenage years, because they've learned they can come to you with their problems.

• • •

•• 17 ••

Show Your Love

"Parental love and valuing is the child's oxygen line."
— *Dorothy Briggs*

Although most parents understand how important love is for the development of a child, it is remarkable how few concrete expressions of love make it into our daily rituals. It is natural for children to sometimes feel insecure since childhood is full of change. Often children have to switch schools or move to a new town or just get used to a new set of friends. Since childhood can be so dynamic it is important that children understand their family's love is constant.

A concrete expression of love that made its way into our family is the "three-way hug." It started when we just had our first child, Michael. When he was upset or just feeling a little sad and a normal hug didn't make him feel better, Mike and I would wrap our arms around him and in a low voice chant, "three-way hug." Michael would join in, and the chant would become quite loud and soon we would all be laughing. When Mitch came along our "three-way hug" became a "four-way hug," and with the addition of Marc it became a "five-way hug." Finally, with the birth of our daughter Meredith, it became a "six-way hug" and the chant and laughter was louder than ever. It's very corny and goofy, but that's why it makes us laugh and forget why we're upset in the first place. More importantly, it is a tradition that encourages an expression of support and solidarity. When you show your love to your children you let them know that you'll always be there for each other and that can make childhood a little easier.

• • •

•• 18 ••

Embrace Friendship

"Of all the things which wisdom provides to make life entirely happy, much the greatest is the possession of friendship."
— *Epicurus*

There are many important things that parents can do to support their children, but it is also important for parents to find ways to support themselves. One of the best ways to make your life a little easier and more enjoyable during the early years of parenting is through friendships. Parents of babies and young children benefit from the companionship and camaraderie of adults they can count on for support, advice and help during these exhausting years. When you have a friend to talk to, the challenges of parenting become less daunting and you find you can meet them with more energy.

I don't know what I would have done without my friend Marilyn Ornstein. I liked her the moment we met more than 20 years ago at a neighborhood block party in Chapel Hill, North Carolina. She was funny, intelligent, interesting and had a little girl named Miriam who was about the same age as our Michael. Over the years our friendship developed as we supported each other through the trials of parenting. Soon Marilyn and her husband, Peter, had their second daughter, and Mike and I had our second boy, Mitchell. Seventeen months later our third child, Marc, arrived. Raising three energetic young boys was not easy, but over the five years that we lived in Chapel Hill, Marilyn and I took care of each other's children and we made parenting fun. When Marilyn and Peter needed a break, we baby-sat for their two gentle girls and in exchange when Mike and I needed a day off, Marilyn and Peter got to experience the joy of three wildly energetic boys. (Not quite an even swap.) We took up new hobbies together, talked about events in the community, and solved the world's problems while breaking up fights in the sandbox. The support of a friend makes all the difference in making sure both you and your children enjoy their childhood.

• • •

•• 19 ••

Be Patient

"An error means a child needs help, not a reprimand or ridicule for doing something wrong."
— *Marva Collins*

Support can take many forms. Often people think of support as something you do for your children, but support is also a state of mind. When parents are patient with their children they allow them to feel secure as they develop and that makes childhood more enjoyable.

I'm a type-A personality. This has helped me with the energy, stamina and resourcefulness you need to raise four active children, but it does have its drawbacks. My greatest challenge has always been developing patience.

A few years back, one of our friends lent us their beach house for the Easter weekend. I wanted to make sure we had a fun Easter celebration so I had gone out the night before and bought two dozen eggs and a set of colored dyes. The morning we left, I placed the eggs in a bag with the dyes and put them in the back of our Caravan on top of the luggage. A few hours later, we piled all the kids in and left for the beach house. It was a long drive and when we finally arrived we were all eager to get inside. As I was unlocking the door to the house I heard Meredith yell, "Oh no, Mom is going to kill me!" I ran over to the car and there was Meredith standing next to a pile of broken eggs.

Apparently in her rush to get her luggage out of the car she had knocked the bag full of eggs onto the driveway. Normally, I would have yelled at her, she would have yelled back and soon the whole day would have been ruined. But at that moment I remembered how important it was for me to work on my patience. I took a deep breath, waited a few seconds and said, "Don't worry, I know you didn't mean it. Let's just get the luggage inside so we can enjoy the beach." It is easy to let a little accident spoil your day. Everyone makes careless mistakes. This is especially true of children. One of the best ways parents can make childhood a little easier is to develop a patient state of mind.

• • •

•• 20 ••

Be Aware

"How can one grasp the dimensions of a spacious house from the perspective of a person sitting in a well?"

— *Hui-lin*

An important part of parenting is keeping your eyes and ears open. In order to guide your children through life you must constantly be aware of their feelings and use this information to anticipate future problems.

When our children were little we had a large group of friends in Greenfield, Massachusetts who often invited us to their homes for family events. On one particularly hectic weekend, we had received four different invitations, one right after the other. Friday night was a barbecue at the Buenos', Saturday morning was a little league breakfast, and on Saturday night we attended a Burns' birthday party. By the time Sunday afternoon rolled around our whole family was a bit tired, but I had accepted an invitation to the Bersons' family softball game.

At noon I went around the house to make sure everyone was ready to leave. When I got to the living room I found Marc, then three, fast asleep on the couch. I touched him gently on the shoulder. Marc looked up and in a meek voice said, "Mom, I don't want to go." Ignoring his exhaustion, I picked him up and gave him a piggy-back ride over to the Bersons' house. Marc got down and slowly made his way over to our friends' children. I went in to help Ellen bring out the food and two minutes later I heard our friend Dan Davis let out a yell. I came running out to see what had happened and found Dan jumping around with Marc's teeth firmly attached to his leg. It seems Dan had taken a bat away from Marc, and Marc, deluded by exhaustion, responded by biting him. I should have been aware that Marc was just too exhausted for one more social event and what he needed instead was a nice long nap. By being aware of your child's physical and emotional needs many potential problems can be avoided.

• • •

Theme #3
INVOLVE

Active participation is the catalyst that moves all human development forward. The principle of involvement encourages the exploration of new worlds and the development of new relationships. It applies to both family and friends, parents and children, and communities and their residents. It motivates parents to find the time to be involved with their children in projects and it urges children to involve grandparents in their lives. It encourages parents to participate in the development of their communities, and communities to participate in the development of their children. In short, the principle of involvement reaffirms the belief that experience is important and that exposure to new ideas, whether they come from a favorite aunt or a treasured book, help both child and parent develop to their full potential.

• • •

·· 21 ··

Be Responsible

"You have no control over other people, the weather and many life events. But you can control what you think and do in the present to deal with situations."
— *Eileen Shiff*

Parents will always have to accept a great deal of responsibility since their role in their child's development is so crucial. There will be times when this responsibility leads parents to choose between their plans and the needs of their child. When these conflicts arise it is important to take a step back and focus on the most important issue, the well-being of your child.

One night, as Mike and I were getting ready to leave for a play, I heard Mitchell exclaim, "Oh my God, I just erased my term paper!" I found him with his head buried against the keyboard. He had been working on this paper for a week and just as he was finishing it up he had accidentally erased it. All that was left were a few pages of notes and Mitch's recollection of what he had written. It was Sunday night and the paper was due the next day. To make matters worse, Mitch was just learning to type and I knew that at his slow pace he would never finish the paper on time. I looked at Mike. We had bought tickets for the winter play in Springfield a month in advance. He didn't have to say a word. We both walked over to the front closet and put our coats away. That night Mitch dictated his paper as I typed. Over the next four hours, slowly but surely, his term paper was raised from the dead. We printed out the paper, stapled it and placed it on the kitchen table. As we headed up to bed Mitch turned to me and said, "Thanks, Mom, I know you didn't have to do that. I don't know what I would have done without your help." Many times along the path of development your child will need your help. It is important as we make plans and fill our calendars to remember that our children are more important than any play or night out with friends. We are their parents and with that title comes responsibility.

• • •

•• 22 ••

Set the Stage

"We must have a place where children can have a whole group of adults they can trust."
— *Margaret Mead*

Parents of young children often find themselves torn between their desire to spend time with their adult friends and the need to spend time with their children. The time constraints on most parents today are enormous. They often feel they don't have enough time. So, when they spend time with their friends they feel guilty that they are not with their children, and when they spend time with their children they resent not being able to spend time with their friends. In order to resolve this difficult problem it is important that you "set the stage" by surrounding yourself with friends that involve children in the activities.

There is nothing that will endear me more to any adult than to see him playing with a child or doing something nice for a child. So it was easy for Mike and I to make friends with Tony and Marie Van Dyke when our kids were little. Tony and Marie managed to create a whole new family social scene for anyone with whom they came in contact. Their greatest joy was setting up fun things for both their friends and their children to do together. The week before Halloween they always held a big pumpkin-carving party. In the spring they led a hike to a local pond where we caught frogs for the county frog-jumping contest. In the summer they would hold a make-your-own-pasta party, and in the winter, a holiday bash. Whatever they did they always made sure that it was fun for kids and adults. Their "kid-friendly" get-togethers eased the tension between time spent with our friends and time spent with our children since our children became part of these social gatherings. Everyone with children should have at least one set of friends like Tony or Marie. Look for them. They're out there.

• • •

•• 23 ••

Participate in Your Community

"It takes a whole village to raise a child."
—*African saying*

One of our greatest challenges today is to follow our finer instincts, despite the often overwhelming demands on our time and energy.

It was one week before Halloween, and my nephew Matthew ran into the kitchen to announce that he had finally decided what he wanted to be for Halloween. My sister-in-law Diana spent the next few days cutting and sewing until his costume was complete.

"Matt," she told him. "I'm all done with your costume. Don't forget to pick up your UNICEF box at school."

"But my school isn't doing it this year," he replied.

Diana was startled.

"Matt, are you sure? I'll check with your principal."

Sure enough, the principal hadn't been able to find anyone to distribute the UNICEF boxes and help count the money. So they had decided not to participate. Diana did not hesitate for a second. She volunteered to be responsible for the distribution and collection of the UNICEF boxes. The program was important to her. She wanted to make sure that her children and the children of her community did not miss out on this opportunity to think of others.

Needless to say, the next forty-eight hours were quite hectic, as she gathered her friends to help get the boxes to the children on time. So many telephone calls to make, pick-ups, deliveries, and then the counting and rolling of all those coins! Everyone pitched in, and Matt was amazed to see how many rolls of coins they had collected.

Diana's "I'll do it" response came from her compassionate heart, rather than her logical mind, reminding us of how we'd like to think we'd respond when we see a need. Over and over again, I have seen the good that one person can do and how it can affect so many lives.

Our children need us to help them find opportunities to practice their roles in their community—and they need our examples to reinforce their finer instincts.

• • •

•• 24 ••

Connect the Generations

*"The continuity of all cultures depends on the living presence
of at least three generations."*
— *Margaret Mead*

Grandparents can contribute so much to the development of a child. Sadly, the last few decades have been a period marked by an increasing separation of the generations. At a time when there are more single-parent households and an increasing number of families where both parents work, older generations are an untapped resource that can no longer be overlooked.

Grandparents are invaluable when you are in need of a helping hand, but their support also takes subtler, more important forms. Some of my children's most enduring childhood memories are of the times we spent at my mother's house. In the fall we would all arrive for our annual leaf-raking. We would awaken early to rake up the leaves around the house from the tall maple trees that lined the street. Everyone helped out, even the littlest child. I can still picture my sister Priscilla's 3-year-old,

Maria, pushing one lone leaf with her itty-bitty rake. To keep the day fun we would take frequent breaks to drink coffee and cider and snack on donuts.

While her children and grandchildren cleaned up the lawn my mother would prepare a great dinner. During the day the grandchildren would often go into the house for visits with their grandmother. After one of these fall weekends, as we were pulling out of the driveway, Mitchell said to me, "Grandma is too delicious!" We all laughed and I rolled down the car window to share this compliment with my mom. "Mom, Mitchell just said you were too delicious." As we pulled onto the main road Mitchell tugged at my sleeve and whispered, "Mom, I said Grandma's too *religious.*" I guess my mom was giving her grandchildren religious instruction throughout the day, too.

There are many ways that grandparents can help in the development of your child, but the most important thing they provide is a continuity of culture. By sharing with your children the wisdom they shared with you, your parents bring each generation together.

• • •

• • 25 • •

Be Creative

"Creation, even when it is a mere outpouring from the heart, wishes to find a public. By definition, creation is sociable."
— *Lu Xun*

Creativity brings people together. Activities that require imagination or encourage artistic expression are a perfect opportunity to involve yourself in your child's growth.

My sister, Penny, loves to create imaginative settings for family and friends. A few years ago Mike and I were traveling down the East Coast and decided to stop at Penny's house in Delaware to drop off birthday gifts for our twin nieces, Maggie and Erin, who three weeks earlier had turned 6 years old. As we pulled into the driveway we heard children's voices singing, "We're off to see the Wizard, the wonderful Wizard of Oz," coming from the garage. We got out of the car and made our way to the window. I looked in and there were my nieces with a group of neighborhood children dressed as the characters in *The Wizard of Oz*. My sister had painted a yellow brick road down the middle of the garage floor and there was a box painted green and covered in green sparkling glitter, a beautiful rendition of the Emerald City. When we walked into the garage we noticed a huge rainbow made of colored tissue paper on the ceiling. "What's this?" I asked. My sister explained that they had been reading *The Wizard of Oz* and she decided to use it as the theme for this year's birthday party. Three weeks later, the neighborhood children were still enjoying the make-believe world Penny had created for her children's party.

Being creative with your children does not have to be so dramatic. When our children were growing up in New England we turned those log-cabin-fever days of winter into a time for simple projects with the children. Sometimes we would make homemade pasta together and let the children mix the ingredients and turn the pasta press. Other days we would make simple piñatas with strips of paper and liquid starch placed over a balloon. There are many activities you can do with your children. The important thing is to encourage them to be creative and to use the activities to bring your family together.

• • •

Be Active in Your School

"A child miseducated is a lost child."
— *John F. Kennedy*

As parents we all have responsibilities. Often we think of these responsibilities as limited to our own children. But as our children grow older it becomes much more difficult to separate the well-being of our children from the well-being of the community. Healthy communities make healthy children, and the most important institution in a healthy community is the school.

Greenfield, Massachusetts was a school district limited in financial resources, but not in human resources when we moved there in 1978. I was soon drawn to an organization called "The Volunteers in the Public Schools." The parents in this organization set up reading programs, science centers, family nights, teacher appreciation night, and a wide variety of activities that supplemented the resources of the classroom. I used to get my whole family involved in an annual event we called

"Saturday Morning Live." It was an interactive Children's Fair with all sorts of booths and activities for the children to explore.

By coming together to support the community all of the parents involved helped their children in a way they could not have done as individuals. Children need healthy communities and communities can't be healthy without the support of its parents. Everyone wins. Volunteering in the classroom is a wonderful way to get to know the teachers and curriculum. Parental support helps the teachers create the best environment for their students. And best of all, by supporting your community you can assure that your children grow up in the healthy environment they deserve.

• • •

•• 27 ••

Be a Resource

"The world
For whose sake does it exist?
For the sake of the little ones
Of all places, of all times . . ."
— *Saul Tchernichovsky*

From the moment little babies are born they count on their parents to create a happy and stimulating world. They can't look at interesting things if someone doesn't set up different things for them to look at. They can't learn how to grab unless they're given rattles to reach for. Children enter this world with a wide variety of aptitudes and huge potential but they will never discover what they are unless parents provide the opportunity to explore, create and imagine through a wide variety of materials and adventures.

Years ago I walked over to my friend Marilyn's house to give her some extra pillows she had asked to borrow for her weekend guests. I called out to her and didn't get an answer so I decided to put the pillows in her kitchen.

As I put them on a chair I heard Marilyn moan, "I have no place to put this stuff." I poked my head into her downstairs bathroom and there on the floor were cardboard toilet paper rolls, tissue boxes, oatmeal boxes, and a wide assortment of old wrapping paper and ribbons. Marilyn used her second shower stall as a mini-recycling center for all her children's creative projects. Peter, her husband, decided a second bathroom was needed for weekend guests. I laughed at Marilyn's predicament because her household was so child-oriented. My children always loved going to her house because Marilyn was such a resource for their projects.

Whether your children are 14 months old or 14 years old, learning occurs best in a resource-rich environment. The resource may be building materials in a variety of shapes, textures and colors, or it may be a pencil sharpener permanently screwed to a sturdy desk with a good study lamp. Being a resource for your children is all about thinking ahead and taking actions to create a positive learning environment.

• • •

•• 28 ••

Promote Home Literacy

"The best friend a person can have is reading and writing."
— *Hojo Soun*

One of my fondest and most tender memories of our children growing up was watching them listen to Mike read a series of books called, *The Box Car Children.* Each night they'd all hop on our bed and Mike would stretch out as they all took a place under his arms. Night after night they couldn't wait to find out what would happen next in these adventures.

Six years ago we sent our oldest son, Michael, off to college. As we were packing all the stuff he would need, he turned to me and said, "Mom, do you still have all those books you used to read to me like, *Where the Wild Things Are?*" Michael was making sure we did not give away all those picture books. These were the books that were there when he was tucked into bed. These were the treasures of his childhood. Now that the children are older, I sometimes purchase a new copy of a favorite classic as a special birthday gift.

Wouldn't it be wonderful if children never knew a day without books, if babies arrived home from the hospital and the first gift to arrive was a bundle of books all tied up in a bow? We really would be handing our children the gift of reading on a silver platter.

I was walking through Marc's room recently and noticed all the fascinating books on his shelves. I thought to myself, "He'll never be lonely." The way many approach reading is as a chore, when really it's all about expanding horizons, companionship and satisfying natural curiosity.

• • •

Share Your Values

"While we don't have a right to impose our values on our children, as parents we do have the responsibility to share our values with them."

— *Thomas Lickona*

There's a saying that "civilization is just the slow process of learning to be kind." Over many centuries the progress of the human race has occurred within the family structure with parents carefully defining principles and reinforcing them with lessons and examples for everyday life.

Every Christmas since our children were little, Mike would take the time to search for a quote or theme that would remind him of a strength of one of our children or an example of a value that he wanted to share with them. He would go to the local card store and purchase cards with space on the front. Then he would carefully print a message and put it in a small frame for each one. The last thing he would do was place it on their dresser on

Christmas Eve. This was his gift to our children. It was the first gift they saw as they awoke on Christmas morning. Even Meredith, when she was 3, awoke to a little message on Christmas morning: the story of a robin who helped an animal in the forest. The message read, "A little kindness goes a long way."

If our children do not learn from us, then from whom will they learn values? From television? From strangers? From other children? In order for our children to learn values, they must see that our lives reflect our stated beliefs. Words are not enough. It is our actions – how our time is spent and what type of role models we are – that makes the difference. It is through these actions that we help define the values they will inherit.

• • •

•• 30 ••

Work Together

"To know how to do something well is to enjoy it."
— *Pearl Buck*

The history of the human family has always included work. Built into our fabric is the expectation that members of a family will unite and function so that the whole is greater than the sum of the parts. Whether in a rural setting or in a city this ability to come together has helped define family success. More than that, working together toward a common goal has defined the family itself.

On one long, hot, muggy day, all of our kids (our daughter-in-law included) were lying on the grass, bronzed from a full day of hard work painting our house. I couldn't believe that they were still joking around and were still in good spirits after such an exhausting day. Our grown children had come home together to help us paint our house.

This type of family spirit was something I remembered from the past when the kids were young. Each fall, several days before Thanksgiving, cords of wood would be dumped in our driveway in New England. The kids would form a line as we passed the wood to the last person who would stack it one on top of another. The kids would keep standing next to it to see if they were still taller than the stack. There was always a sense of teamwork, camaraderie and accomplishment. Coming together around hard work and involving the whole family strengthened the ties among us.

In today's world most of the forces draw people apart and encourage individuality over teamwork. Sometimes you have to work hard to define activities and experiences that bring family together. We could have hired professional painters who would have done the job in half the amount of time. But in doing it together we found time for each other and created an album of memories. Every time I drive up to the house these days, I think of our kids together again. A job well done!

• • •

Theme #4
PLAN

In order to make the most of your parenting years you have to think ahead. Planning requires a special mixture of vision and vigilance. You must open your mind to many different possibilities for the future and then follow through in the present. This principle of planning begins with parents' preparation for the birth of their child and continues through childhood and adolescence. It encourages parents to preserve the past through the collection of their child's drawings and to provide an age appropriate environment by becoming better informed. Most of all, this principle urges parents to plan for success by creating the opportunities that their children will need in order to reach their goals. However, the principle of planning is more than what you can do for your child. By developing your children's ability to plan you prepare them to do for themselves, and that is something that will carry them forward throughout their lives.

• • •

•• 31 ••

Be Prepared

*"You must create your own world. I am responsible
for mine."*

— *Louise Nevelson*

The first step parents must take to support their children
is to plan for their birth. Planning helps you work
through any problems beforehand and gives you more
free time once your child has arrived. Preparation not
only allows your child to experience a better, more well-
thought-out environment, but it allows you to experience
the fun of creating an environment for your child without the stress of having to both create it and take care of
your child at the same time.

During our first few years of marriage Mike and I
lived in Syracuse, New York. Mike was a medical student
and I taught first grade. Two months after we were married we found out I was pregnant. We had hardly any
money and lived in a small student- housing apartment.
That winter was particularly harsh and the snow just

seemed to keep coming. Despite these conditions, and perhaps because of them, we decided one weekend after a huge snow storm to prepare for our first child by remaking our apartment. We talked our friends into going to the lumberyard with us and buying a 4 foot by 8 foot piece of 1/4 -inch plywood to make animals for our new nursery. We spent the entire weekend drawing, sawing and painting dozens of life-size animals to transform the old side room into a nursery. We played music and sang as we worked throughout the weekend on the room. When we had finished painting scenery on the walls and had nailed the wooden animals in place, we took an old family crib, painted it bright yellow and set it right in the middle of our new nursery. What had started out as a responsibility turned into one of our most enjoyable weekends in Syracuse. Somewhere along the line, as we created that environment, we had shaken off the winter blues.

Shortly after Michael was born I received a visit from a public health nurse. It was standard procedure at that time to visit all the babies born in our zip code since it was such a poor area. She asked if she could see the baby and also see what sleeping space we provided. If I only had a camera that day to capture the astonished look on her face as I opened the door to Michael's room to reveal the bright colors of the animated jungle. She stood there for a few seconds with her mouth wide open and then exclaimed that it was the most amazing thing she had ever seen. She said it must have taken a tremendous amount of work, but as I thought back on the weekend we spent creating it, all I could remember was the fun.

From the moment I found out we were expecting a baby I had a desire to create a special world for him. Once it was built, I would tuck Michael in bed each night by saying good night to those animals. We had created a fun environment for our baby by planning ahead and in doing so we made it fun for ourselves.

• • •

•• 32 ••

Preserve the Past

"What is not recorded is not remembered."
— *Benazir Bhutto*

Too often in our society the past goes unexamined and uncelebrated. This is not just a problem that should be addressed by history professors. The preservation of the past should be equally supported by families.

A few years ago, my daughter, Meredith, gave a bridal shower for our daughter-in-law, Susanna, who was engaged to our oldest son, Michael. It was a wonderful affair because the whole family was able to gather together to welcome Susanna into the family. Both grandmothers were there along with lots of aunts and cousins. One of the last gifts Susanna opened was a beautifully bound leather album that Mike's mother had painstakingly put together. The album documented the history of the Magee family with narrative and photographs. Susanna's face lit up as she turned the pages saying things like, "Oh, this is so wonderful to have," and "I will treasure this always." She finally turned to the last page and there was a picture of her added to the family tree and beneath the picture it read, "Welcome to our family. Love, Grandma Magee." Susanna burst into tears, and as the book was passed around, soon there wasn't a dry eye in the room.

There are many different ways parents can preserve the past. When my kids were preschoolers I used to sit them on my lap and we would look at their baby books together. Every few weeks we would put a new photograph or drawing into the book. Over the years they have continued to add to their books and always enjoy looking through them and rediscovering the past. By preserving the past you help your children appreciate where they came from and that helps them understand where they're going.

• • •

•• 33 ••

Set Up Routines

"Order is the shape upon which beauty depends."
— *Pearl S. Buck*

Some people confuse having routines with being rigid. But where rigidity brings discomfort to people, routine carries predictable comfort. Others think of routines as boring, and while too much routine can destroy spontaneity, the right amount can reinforce traditions in a pleasing way.

One night, as we were finishing washing the dishes, I announced, "It's time to put Meredith to bed." Marc, then 6, went over to our 1-year-old Meredith and said, "Okay, Meredith, it's time to put on your bedtime marching shoes." He bent down and pretended to put on "the bedtime marching shoes." This was a routine that we made up years ago that would transition our three active little boys from playtime to bedtime. Each night they would take a turn leading the march to bed. We would make up a marching song and off we'd go for bath, stories and bed.

Routines are successful patterns worth preserving. Having routines means your child will have a general framework of predictability that reinforces personal security. Within that comfort zone, our children found the freedom to imagine and explore.

• • •

• • 34 • •

Celebrate Uniqueness

"It is not necessary for eagles to be crows."
— *Sitting Bull*

While all children want to be accepted by the group, the desire to be individuals runs at least as strongly. The subtleties and complexities of human life are so obvious that even the youngest of children understand their uniqueness. Each is an individual. Each is different in how they see themselves and the world around them. Recognizing a child's uniqueness is part of a parent's responsibility.

Sometimes the easiest way to do this is to go back to the beginning, to the day your child was born. Birthdays are a great time to focus on the individual, the day and time of the birth, the circumstances, choosing a name, and sharing the way you feel about your child. Birthdays were a very big day in my house. My mother always put up a big sign with my name on it. We've continued the tradition in our house, taking it one step further. Using a large roll of computer paper we create a sign 12 inches wide and 10 feet long. In large balloon letters we write

"HAPPY BIRTHDAY" and then everyone uses magic markers to convert the letters into animated characters and creatures with special greetings coming out of their mouths. Once done the banner is hung across one wall and it stays up about a week. We began this when the kids were young and the tradition hasn't died. I wouldn't be surprised if the celebration banner carries on to the next generation. Celebrating uniqueness says "You're special!"

• • •

• • 35 • •

Be Knowledgeable

*"Parental love is as natural as rain, parenting skills
need to be taught."*

— *William Raspberry*

As parents we need to recognize that parenting a child
requires knowledge as well as love and dedication. We
need to take what we have gained by instinct and example and support it by thought, discussion and reflection.
Children are complicated and each child is different.
Add to this that every child is a living, breathing, developing piece of art, constantly evolving and constantly
reaching out for understanding.

A few years ago as I was perusing the parenting section of our local bookstore, my eyes caught the title of a
book, *Raising Your Spirited Child.* I went on to read the
subtitle, *A Guide for Parents Whose Child is More Intense,
Sensitive, Perceptive, Persistent, Energetic.* "Hmm, that
sounds like my Marc," I said aloud. I purchased the book
and spent the next week absorbed in the information

that would change my attitude about parenting. This book helped me see Marc in a totally different light. Yes he was more of everything. When I thought about it he was more responsible, more tenderhearted, more curious and definitely more energetic. I found myself reflecting on the time when our boys were each given two dollars to participate in the school holiday bazaar. Within 15 minutes my oldest two sons had traded their money for an assortment of treasures. But nearly two hours later Marc was hard at work still deliberately searching for the perfect purchase. At my wits' end, I searched down the aisles, spotted him and could feel my temper rising. But as he ran toward me, he held up a package and yelled, "Mom, I bought you a present." I opened it and there was a pair of earrings. It was my birthday that day and he had spent all of his money on a gift for me.

Most of us seek out advice from other parents and friends, from teachers and siblings. But there is also an increasing amount of excellent written materials on parenting. I think every adult could benefit from a child development course whether or not they have children. When you think about how the teachers who work in child-care settings need many courses and experiences before they're prepared to play with and care for children, doesn't it seem reasonable that parents would benefit from the same knowledge?

• • •

•• 36 ••

Be Visionary

"Tomorrow is now."

— *Eleanor Roosevelt*

Children are so active and engaged, they naturally see life in the "now." This creates a wonderful sense of vibrancy and presence that is part of the joy of parenthood. But at the same time parents need to teach their children that the present is attached to the future and that tomorrow's future is tied to today's actions.

Every spring, when the kids were young, I would head on over to *Knapp's Hardware Store* with all of them and let everyone pick out a packet of vegetable seeds. They would carefully carry home their packets and proudly plant the seeds, tenderly patting the ground overhead as they "put them to bed." For the next couple of weeks we would hoe and dig and water and fertilize until one of the kids would see the very first sprout of our efforts. We would then watch the plants carefully to make sure that weeds or insects weren't destroying any of our plantings. To keep the kids interested in the garden we would envision how big our pumpkins would grow, or how long the cucumbers would become, or guess how many tomatoes would grow on one vine. Year after year the kids noticed that whenever we put a lot of time into our garden we would have big baskets of vegetables to eat. The years we forgot to water or were just too lazy to pull away the weeds, we had very few vegetables to pick.

When children learn to look ahead, they develop the skills to help them take control over their futures. It is in seeing the connection between today and tomorrow that they understand the real work that is necessary to realize their dreams.

• • •

•• 37 ••

Plan for Success

"Put your heart, mind, intellect and soul even to your small-
est acts. This is the secret of success."
— *Sivananda Sarasvati*

Most parents are very focused on making certain their children hear "the message." We feel if all those words stick then perhaps success will follow. But a child's sense of self-worth and success often comes from symbolic quests and emotions released when a good idea is well executed.

One Saturday morning in August, I saw Mike and Marc lugging an old oak desk out of our station wagon. It was time to start thinking about school again. Mike had been helping Marc get the needed supplies for school when they passed a flea market. Marc had eyed this beat-en-up desk and said, "Dad, I'd like that desk for my room." It was dirty and old but Marc must have loved the bigness of it. So Mike agreed on a price and there it stood on our front lawn. Over the next several days, Mike and Marc worked on cleaning, sanding and staining the desk until it satisfied them both. A few days before school began, they carried the desk up to Marc's room and bought a green banker's lamp for the desktop. I think that desk set the stage for Marc's attitude about studying that year. It was an important piece of furniture to his room. I noticed he would occasionally run his hand across the top of the desk to feel the smooth grain. He genuinely smiled when he sat down to study.

How comfortable your child feels in their environment is determined by the little things. So keep an eye out for opportunities to reinforce positive behavior from the first day of life.

• • •

•• 38 ••

Encourage Goals

"To climb steep hills requires a slow pace at first."
— William Shakespeare

Life is full of challenges, small and large, that we must learn to face and overcome. It is in this pursuit of solutions to their problems that children learn the importance of setting of goals from parents and teachers.

As a teacher, there are little children in your life that you never forget. One such child was a little girl named Patty. I was her first grade teacher and she never ceased to inspire me. The curriculum of the first grade did not come easily to Patty. Twenty-eight years ago my class was required to read from a basal reader that described a perfectly intact household living in a lovely house with a white picket fence. I think she had trouble relating to the material because she came from one of the few single-parent families in our school and from a family that struggled daily to make ends meet. There were also learning issues that prevented her from easily reading the stories.

Each day Patty put all of her energy, determination and attention into doing her work.

One day I sat her down and told her how proud I was of her. "But, Mrs. Magee," She said, "I take so much longer than everyone else and I never get everything right."

"Patty," I replied, "you have the secret ingredients to make all your dreams come true because you are such a hard worker, and you're so cooperative and you never give up. I know you are going to become whatever you want to be."

Many years later I bumped into her mom at a department store and of course asked about Patty. "Mrs. Magee, you won't believe this. She's on the honor roll at high school." I replied, "Oh, yes I would!"

By assisting a child in visualizing a goal, a parent gently sets an expectation that success will follow. But more than that, the process expresses your confidence in your child's ability.

• • •

•• 39 ••

Prepare to Learn

*"Learning is not attained by chance. It must be sought for
with ardor and attended to with diligence."*
— *Abigail Adams*

Parents will inevitably have a great deal of influence on
the living and learning environments of their children.
By what they choose to invest in, how they organize
materials, and the amount of time they set aside for inter-
action, they determine their child's readiness to learn.

Our first apartment in Syracuse was furnished at a
fire sale at the Salvation Army. Our dining room chairs
cost $1 each and we thought the wrinkled fire marks gave
an antique look to all the furniture we had bought. With
such a frugal mentality about our furnishings, our
friends were quite surprised when I ordered a large set of
wooden blocks for Michael for $57. Those blocks
became the centerpiece for all learning, creating and
imagining in our home during his early years. On rainy
Saturday mornings those blocks were dragged out and

Mitch, Marc and Mike would spend hours creating speedways, castles or whatever.

Life is all about setting priorities. By making learning an early and important priority for your family, you ensure your child's well-rounded growth and at the same time, ensure that a philosophy of learning will be part of your child's inheritance.

• • •

•• 40 ••

Encourage Independence

*"No one can build their security upon the nobleness
of another person."*

— *Willa Cather*

Letting go is not something that comes naturally to parents. Because so much of what we do for our children involves providing protection and support, it is easy to forget how important it is for children to learn to do for themselves. One of the most important things you can give your child is the gift of independence.

"Mom, can I have $11 for the PSATs?" Meredith called to me from upstairs one day. I thought maybe she didn't understand that PSATs were taken during junior year. "Meredith, you don't have to take those until next year," I said. "I know, but I just want to try this year to see how I do."

This independent spirit took root long ago when I learned to step back and allow Meredith to take charge of her own affairs and do things the way she wanted. When she was little we set up her room so hooks were low enough that she could hang up her own clothes. When she was older we purchased a bulletin board so she could tack up reminders of the things she had to do and we also let her bear the consequences for things like forgetting to do her homework.

Encouraging independence requires different strategies for different children. Clearly, some are more prepared to accept responsibility than others. But by setting up the expectation for independence, supporting personal growth and reinforcing individual success when it occurs you help build the foundations for future independence.

• • •

Theme #5
ENJOY

It is important, above all else, to remember that parenting should be fun. This does not mean that all problems can be avoided. Parenting will inevitably have its highs and lows. Instead, the principle of enjoyment encourages parents to rethink any environment in which they are unable to enjoy their children. In addition, it urges parents to embrace celebration and adventure. When you enjoy parenting you demonstrate a positive attitude toward life, and in so doing, become a positive role model for your children. This can take the form of finding more play time during the week or going on a spontaneous picnic on a nice summer day. Lastly, the principle of enjoyment reminds us of the importance of humor in everyday life. Enjoyment brings everyone in the family closer together because it builds relationships that are valued and creates shared experiences that all members of the family will treasure.

• • •

•• 41 ••

Have Fun

"You teach your child the value of fun when you demonstrate a positive attitude toward life."

— *Eileen Shiff*

Often when parents set up activities to do with their children they end up more work than fun. When an activity has turned into a chore, look to your child to set the right tone. If their is adventure in an activity, children will always find it.

Making cookies with your children, what could be a more warm, happy activity? One cold autumn day I decided that it would be fun to make a batch of chocolate chip cookies. I gathered my three little boys around our kitchen table and, after assembling the ingredients, we all took turns measuring, pouring and stirring. The kids quickly went to work as they moved rambunctiously from step to step. Before long they had eaten most of the chocolate chips and the dozen eggs had fallen on the floor. I tried desperately to hold the activity together. I gave commands left and right. "Stop that! Put those down! Don't put your hands there!" The more I yelled, the more the activity disintegrated. Finally, Mitchell tapped me on the shoulder and said, "Mom, why are we doing this if it isn't any fun?"

I had lost sight of why I was making chocolate chip cookies with my children in the first place. It wasn't about improving on Mrs. Fields, it was about spending time together. From that day forward whenever I did any activity with my children I kept in mind the old educational theory, "process not product." The joy is in the creating. After that, whenever we made a batch of cookies, we never ended up with more than five or six in the oven, but we had a great time licking the batter, singing a clean-up song when we made a big mess, and making sure we had plenty of time to enjoy the activity together.

• • •

•• 42 ••

Be Adventurous

"We live in a wonderful world that is full of beauty and charm and adventure. There is no end to the adventures that we can have if only we seek them with our eyes open."
— *Jawaharlal Nehru*

Often parents think that they must go somewhere special in order for their children to have a fun learning experience. But in reality, every environment can be an adventure for a child and the best place to start is in your own neighborhood.

It started out as a typical day with Michael, then 2 years old. He had become bored with the usual activities so I decided that for a break we would just walk around the neighborhood. We made our way out onto the street and as I turned the corner of our apartment complex I noticed huge equipment that was parked near a vacant lot. There were a lot of people walking around with hard hats on. Michael became so excited by the sight that I stopped and asked the construction workers if they could tell us the names of the machines. Michael stood there silent and wide-eyed as they named every piece of equipment: cranes, dump trucks, back hoes, jackhammers and cement trucks. We then spent the next half hour just watching each piece of equipment in action. We watched the workers dig up portions of the road and then fill them back in again with the large cement truck. For Michael, whose favorite toys were his Tonka trucks, it was a dream come true.

After watching the construction for about 20 minutes, we walked over to the library and found some great picture books on trucks. Michael eagerly pointed out what he had seen. We continued down a few more city blocks and I noticed an open air farmers market. We walked along the booths naming all the fruits and vegetables. Along the way we asked the farmers the names of fruit we hadn't seen before and we each got an apple. Next we made our way to the park. When we got there Michael quickly ran toward the big slide. As he made his way to the top I noticed there was a huge puddle of mud at the bottom of the slide. "Michael," I shouted, "don't go down the slide." He was having too much fun to hear my plea and he stepped onto the slide and flew right into the puddle of mud. He stayed in the mud for a while squishing his fingers and toes in the muddy water. Then he looked up and said in a gleeful voice, "I'm going to do that again!" He was already a mess so I thought what the heck. Up and down the slide he went plopping into the muddy puddle. After 15 minutes all I could see were the whites of his eyes. So I picked him up and headed back to our apartment. After a nice warm bath and a few stories about trucks, I tucked him in for a nap. Who would have thought that we could have had such an adventurous day in a four-block radius of our apartment?

• • •

•• 43 ••

Observe

"All the great pleasures in life are silent."
— *George Clemenceau*

Parenting is often frantic, active work. Enjoying your children, however, is easy. All you have to do is stop what you are doing and enjoy the simple pleasure of observation.

A few summers ago, while we were in Cape Cod attending the wedding of one of our nephews, I suggested to Mike that we try to find the old cottage we had rented for our very first family vacation. That afternoon we got in the car and made our way along the familiar roads that led to the bay. As we approached the cottage, I was hit with a rush of emotions as the memories of that first vacation came back to me. That vacation was the first time I was able to leave behind the frenzy of my normal routine and just watch Michael play.

When the tide was out he would run from place to place picking up crabs with a big smile on his face. I would follow him as he walked just out of reach of the waves, stopping sometimes to explore a tide pool, or a little crab left behind by the waves. At the end of the day, as the sun was setting, Michael would gather sand with his little shovel and bucket and then he and Mike would build a sand castle together. Later, we would watch as the waves crashed over the towers and turrets they had built.

As Mike and I walked along the beach 20 years later, I was amazed at the pleasure these memories of watching Michael still brought me. Observation is such a easy thing to do, but it is one of the greatest joys of parenting.

• • •

•• 44 ••

Celebrate

"Be happy. It's one way of being wise."
— *Colette*

One of my greatest joys in life has always been celebrations. They are based on a deceivingly simple concept: organize a gathering under a common theme, bring people together with some decorations and then just have fun. Sometimes in this fast-paced world we need an excuse to take some time off and enjoy each other's company, and that is exactly what celebrations provide.

A few years ago in late October I called my mom to tell her we would be dropping by just to say hi on our way back from a trip to New England. She insisted I plan my stop around dinnertime. I agreed and at 6 pm Mike and I pulled up with a carload of kids. When we walked into the house we were taken aback by an incredible array of decorations. In the dining room orange and black streamers crisscrossed the ceiling and paper jack-o-lanterns were attached to each chair. My mother had prepared a special dinner and afterward we turned off the lights and told ghost stories. That night we all had fun as we participated in the celebration. On the ride home I thought to myself, how does my 76-year-old mom still have the energy and enthusiasm to make each visit special? The more I watch her during these celebrations the more I realize that it is from these events that she draws her energy. They rejuvenate her and make her feel alive.

My mother is and has always been a lot of fun. She loves to have a good time and she loves to celebrate every little event in life. I think it's one of the best gifts she gave to her children. Knowing her story makes this characteristic even more remarkable. When I was 10 years old my father died, leaving my mother at the age of 40 with 10 children, ages 1 through 15. We had very little money and yet I never felt deprived or unhappy. How could I? We were always celebrating something. Our life was filled with constant celebrations. First communions meant white streamers and the table set with a grapefruit with a cherry on top at each place. For birthdays we would make big homemade signs and on Saint Patrick's Day we would decorate the house in green and my mother would serve corn beef and cabbage.

With experiences like these I wasn't surprised when Meredith, age 10, set her alarm one Valentine's day for 5:30 am. She spent the next two hours decorating the kitchen with paper hearts and making heart-shaped pancakes.

I think it takes a lot of effort and energy to create a happy household and celebrations are one way of creating concrete examples of joy.

• • •

• • 45 • •

Take Time to Relax Together

"Your children need your presence more than your presents."
— Jesse Jackson

There are people who believe that leisure time is synonymous with wasting time. Yet taking time to enjoy each other's company, to relax and put aside the demands and anxieties of our everyday work lives, is more important than ever to family life. Recently we were down in Chapel Hill, North Carolina at a reunion, reminiscing about the "good old days" when we were in school and just starting out. Our friends mentioned that one of the things they did then and still do now even though they can afford a more elaborate vacation is trek up by car with a group of friends and stay at an old house by a lake. Their kids still sleep on the floor, chip in and make breakfast, and hike and fish.

At a time in their lives when life was rough and sparse they somehow managed to pool some money together and take their kids on vacation. They managed to create lasting happy memories that their children continue to want to relive even today.

The pendulum is always swinging. You can sense the growing feeling that we need to work more at relaxing than we do at working; more at enjoying, less at succeeding; more at giving, less at getting. If we move to the needs of our children, we are less likely to get off track.

• • •

•• 46 ••

Support Interests

"It is a wise father who knows his own child."
— *William Shakespeare*

While children have a great deal in common, it is important to remember that each child is a unique human being with their own hopes, dreams and interests. One way to support this individuality is by encouraging the activities or programs that attracts your child's interest.

One year, when we were visiting Mike's brother Chris and his wife Christine, I heard my nephew Max's alarm go off at about 6 am. I thought to myself, "My, he gets up early for school." I'm an early riser myself and so I slowly worked my way down to the kitchen to make some coffee. There was Max with his nose in a USA Today newspaper carefully reading the multicolored weather reports of every city in the entire United States. It seems that Max had an intense interest in weather. It absolutely fascinated him. He also had a hard time getting up for school. So Max's parents decided that they would give him a subscription to USA Today for his birthday.

The importance of individual interests includes not only school topics, but also hobbies and even toys. Marc was crazy about super-hero characters when he was a little boy. We had purchased a few of the action figures and he spent hours creating super hero-adventures. That year, as Halloween was approaching, I got out my sewing machine and created an Iron Man costume (his favorite character) out of flannel material. Night after night he wore the Iron Man pajamas until there were two large holes in the knees. We had an Iron Man birthday party that year complete with an Iron Man cake and an Iron man pinata.

By valuing our children's special interests we can show our love for who they are and the special qualities they possess.

• • •

•• 47 ••

Be Thankful

"Gratitude is the heart's memory."
— *French proverb*

It's hard to say why two people can experience the very same set of circumstances, and one feels cheated while the other feels rewarded. Some of it is surely a view of the world that each person carries with her as she enters life. But the rest comes from learning, from watching, from caring for others and from a spirit of gratitude.

My mom was sitting in our backyard one summer day and said aloud, "I have a lot to be thankful for." I was impressed that she could look back on her life with such gratitude after being widowed at age 40 with 10 children. I asked, "Mom, what are you thankful for?" "Well, just look around at all my children and grandchildren, happy and healthy," was her reply.

I remember grocery shopping with my mom one Saturday night when a produce clerk commented on how many children she had and asked what her husband did for a living. "Actually," she said, "I'm a widow." He said, "You know, we discount our produce a dollar a box on Saturday night."

At closing we went back to the produce department and there were several boxes of fruits and vegetables boxed up for us with a dollar sticker stamped on each. We went home that night and made eggplant parmigiana and homemade tomato sauce and other dishes from the overly ripe produce. All the while my mom kept saying how thankful she was that we hit upon this great deal and that we all should say a prayer of thanks for such a nice man.

So the next time you see your child jumping on the couch, first be thankful you have a healthy child with strong legs and then set out to teach her how to sit on the furniture.

• • •

• • 48 • •

Establish Traditions

"The past at least is secure."
— *Daniel Webster*

Traditions remind us of what is constant and stable in our world. In the context of a family these traditions take on a more personal form. They become common memories that tie each family member together through a shared experience. They provide a sense of reliability and security which is constant throughout a child's life. Most importantly, however, they promote the common foundation upon which the family rests.

Tradition can be as simple as a favorite food. I first realized this when our first child, Michael, went off to college. Shortly before his first break we were talking on the phone. After discussing the logistics of getting him home Michael said, "Mom, could you make pot roast when I come home?" For Michael, that familiar dinner gave him a sense of security and consistency with the past. He had missed the atmosphere of our family dinners and his memories became linked with a traditional food.

I think creating a tradition can be as simple as always opening the same brand of chicken soup when your children have a cold or making the same type of cookies each holiday season. These traditions become symbols of your continuous support of them throughout their lives.

• • •

•• 49 ••

Be Spontaneous

"One must scratch the part of the body or mind that itches."
— *Aminu Kano*

Too often in their quest to run well-ordered houses, parents lose sight of the fun of having no plans at all. Routines are important for children, but they should never be allowed to dominate every hour of every day. Sometimes children and parents need to experience the rejuvenating freedom of spontaneity.

Shortly after Michael was born I decided to visit an old college friend named Pat who I hadn't seen in quite awhile. The one thing I remembered most about Pat was how organized she was. However, when I arrived at her house that day something was different. When I walked into the house I noticed dishes stacked up high in the sink and piles of laundry on the floor. I was taken off guard and Pat laughed when she saw my reaction. She said, "How do you like the spontaneous Pat?"

She explained that for 10 days it had been cold and rainy and she and her kids had been stuck indoors.

Everyone had become grumpy and irritable. Finally, the day before I visited, the sun broke through and the cold front passed. She said that she couldn't bear to stay inside with the kids as she had planned in order to finish the house work. Instead, she packed bag lunches, put the kids in the car and headed off toward the local lake. There, under a beautiful blue sky, they built sand castles, read books and just relaxed under the shade of a tree. With a beaming smile she said that it was one of the nicest days she had ever spent with her boys. I could tell by the smiles on their faces that her sons undoubtedly agreed.

• • •

•• 50 ••

Have a Sense of Humor

"Humor is laughing at what you haven't got when
you ought to have it."

— *Langston Hughes*

There will always be challenges and tough times in parenting. Children get sick, there are arguments about grades and bedtimes, and throughout it all is the constant struggle to pay the bills. With all the ups and downs of raising children it is vital that you keep your sense of humor. Laughing is a constant that works equally well in good times and in bad. It relieves stress, gives us a needed break and puts everything in perspective.

When my three boys were little I used to look in the mirror and swear that the bags under my eyes couldn't get any bigger or darker. The next morning I would wake up and be proven wrong. During those first five years I don't think I ever experienced a full night's sleep. In their first few years my three boys seemed to catch every known childhood illness. Those were also the years that Mike was on call every other night as a resident in surgery. He worked a grueling, ever-changing schedule and sometimes I would get so confused I didn't know whether he was across town or just in the other room. One night I heard Mitch crying and jumped up to see what the problem was. As I dashed across the dark hallway to his room I suddenly bonked heads with Mike who was going to another room to assist Michael. I can't explain why, but at that moment we both just looked at each other rubbing our heads and burst into laughter. After a few minutes of laughing we had expressed to each other all the frustration and anxiety we had been feeling and in a much better way than we could have ever done with words.

• • •

POSTSCRIPT

There are so many things a parent must do, so many challenges to overcome, that the task is often overwhelming. How can a parent know if they've done enough? It will not always be possible to remain faithful to all fifty of the principles that have been presented in this book. With love, however, you will find that much that you thought was impossible becomes possible. Love is the foundation upon which you will build your relationship with your child. If you take the time to nurture that love it will guide you through a lifetime of challenges, disappointments, accomplishments and, ultimately, success. As you walk through life with your children, take time out to revisit the experiences you've shared. Your memories of your time together is part of your reward for a life of commitment to your children. Cherish the memories you create as you grow together.

• • •

•• 51 ••

A Parent's Greatest Gift

"Love builds."
— *Mary McLeod Bethune*

There is no question that a baby knows and understands love from her earliest days. You can see it in the newborn's gentle nuzzling in her mother's arms, seeking warmth and comfort, and in the cooing in response to a hug. If you watch a young toddler you can see that the child also understands family love, reaching out with both arms to draw her mother and father closer. A child understands that love builds. This simple observation forms the foundation for successful parenting.

This past summer we celebrated our 25th wedding anniversary with our children in New Hampshire. We awoke on our anniversary to a room filled with balloons and streamers, king and queen hats, and a day of hiking in the White Mountains with our children. They had planned all sorts of activities including a starlit rowboat ride filled with champagne toasts and music. I thought to myself, the greatest gift we've given our children is the security of our love and lifelong commitment to each other, and from our love for each other has grown an unending love for our children.

We learn from our role models. We learn through images repeated and reinforced over many years: images of gentleness, helpfulness, respect, passion and commitment. Love is a great gift. Learned early and reinforced often, it makes all the difference in a child's world.

• • •

•• 52 ••

Create Memories

"Method is the mother of memory."
— *Thomas Fuller*

You and your child will have a long life together. There will be ups and downs, highs and lows, but they will be your experiences, special and sacred to you and your child. Never forget to take time to celebrate what you have shared together. Every year together is an accomplishment, do not let one pass without a celebration for all that has taken place in your trip together through life.

It's strange when your children start to move out of the house. How do you keep the family together when they are geographically apart? A few years ago I saw an advertisement for a family calendar: Send in 12 pictures and a list of important dates in your family and they would create a personal calendar. I went over the pictures of the last year that highlighted some of the times we were all together and sent them off to the company.

I gave the family calendars as Christmas gifts to each of our children and it has rapidly become an important and treasured tradition. Through the calendars we can see our connections with each other, remember each other's birthdays, or just revisit the times we spent together during the previous year.

Within a family's past are trapped a treasure of positive lessons, joyful experiences and hard-fought successes. But families are easily distracted by present events and future demands. So in pictures, words and scrapbooks, preserve those childhood creations. When we celebrate our shared experiences we reinforce our commitment to each other and prepare ourselves for the challenges that await us on the road ahead.

• • •

TRISH MAGEE is an early childhood and parent educator who is currently the director of the *Ready to Learn* program in Philadelphia. She has twenty-seven years of experience as a teacher, college instructor, school board president, and author. She has four children.